This journal belongs to

MIKE CRETARO

....

Date

11/28/22

....

Ellie Claire
Hachette Book Group
1290 Avenue of the Americas, New York, NY 10104
ellieclaire.com

First Edition: June 2019 (hardcover)

Ellie Claire is a division of Hachette Book Group, Inc. The Ellie Claire name and logo are trademarks of Hachette Book Group, Inc.

The publisher is not responsible for websites (or their content) that are not owned by the publisher.

Library of Congress Cataloging-in-Publication Data has been applied for.

Coloring page illustrations by Lizzie Preston courtesy of Advocate Art. Labyrinth art from: Wikimedia Commons: Ssolbergj, commons.wikimedia.org/wiki/File:Labyrinthus.svg and Shutterstock, shutterstock.com.
Print book interior design by Bart Dawson.

ISBN: 978-1-63326-215-7 (hardcover)

Printed in China

RRD

10 9 8 7 6 5 4 3 2 1

Thank you to Pastor Chris Hodges and
the prayer team at Church of the Highlands
for encouraging me to pray regularly,
deeply, and in a variety of creative ways.

Here's the truth:

It's impossible to lack creativity
while standing in the presence of the Creator.
The Lord has graced us with an intrinsic ability
to create. To design beauty from nothing.
To write, to draw, to build,
to sing and to dance for something
and someone bigger than ourselves.

MIKE ROMERO

Contents

Don't worry

about anything; instead,

pray about everything.

Tell God what you need,

and *thank him*

for all he has done.

PHILIPPIANS 4:6 NLT

How to Use This Journal

How many times have you promised yourself or others that you will pray and then didn't? You run out of time, you forget, you don't know what to say… Maybe you are praying regularly but are bored with repeating the same words over and over and want to add some passion and intentionality into your prayer life. Perhaps you have been meaning to pray more regularly and just don't know where to start.

This journal is the answer to all those issues. With fifteen chapters, each suggesting a different creative way to pray, there is something for everyone. From coloring to making lists, from praying through sermon notes to praying through your home, each chapter gives you an example to follow and lots of space to write out prayers, record reactions, or keep track of spiritual disciplines. You may find one chapter is perfect for you today and another works better in a different season of life. Or you may find alternating the chapters throughout the year works wonders for your talks with God. Each chapter is listed in the table of contents under four categories—Art, Place, Bible, Organization—so you can quickly choose the one that works for today.

I searched for creative people who take prayer seriously. I found bloggers, authors, artists, letterers, and creative types who are already using their skills and talents to pray for others. They inspired and encouraged my own prayer life. Some of their ideas and illustrations are included in this book.

Creativity comes from God. He put the creative desires and tendencies in your heart that have led you to journal, scrapbook, sew, paint, sing, dance, make lists, or find joy where others can't. Since He gave it to you, why not use it to draw closer to Him?

Happy journaling,
MARILYN JANSEN
EDITORIAL DIRECTOR, ELLIE CLAIRE

One-Word Prayers

Some folks might think that, for prayers to be effective, they must be long or eloquent. That's not so. Short ones—'Help!'—whispered or cried from a heart that truly recognizes one's need for God's provision or intervention can stir Him to answer," Grace Fox writes on her blog gracefox.com.

Sometimes we just can't find the words to be long and eloquent in prayer. We have no words or no words that make sense—especially when we are overwhelmed with grief, overcome with gratitude, or stunned by a grand gesture. One-word prayers are all we can manage. There are times when "Jesus!" is the only word we can think to pray, and it is enough. Petitioning Him simply and exclusively in this way reveals the need in our hearts.

One-word prayers can be the beginning of a divine communication that transforms our prayer lives and leaves us listening for answers instead of listing demands. Once a week, try taking one word, such as HELP, THANKS, REVEAL, REDEEM, GUIDE, WOW, or FORGIVE, and use that in prayer. "Help me. Help my faith. Help my family. Help me at work. Help so-and-so…" Write the word on a notecard where you pray or put it in your planner to focus on throughout the day. Be creative and letter your word in fancy script, use pretty stickers, or cut letters from a magazine.

By keeping your prayer simple and open-ended, you open the lane of possibility and faith to see how God will answer. His answers may surprise and delight you or give you a change of direction that is just what you need.

Lord, help! Just help! I am at a loss for words. So please hear my sighs, my groans, my cries, and send help! Thank You for listening and helping. You never fail even when my words do. Thank You, Lord.

The prayer of a Christian is not an attempt to force God's hand,
but a humble acknowledgment of helplessness and dependence.

J. I. PACKER

....
....
....
....
....
....
....
....
....
....
....
....
....
....
....
....
....
....
....
....
....
....
....
....
....
....

Your Father knows exactly what you need even before you ask him!

MATTHEW 6:8 NLT

Let us come boldly to the throne of our gracious God. There we will receive his mercy, and we will find grace to help us when we need it most.

"Lord, help!" they cried in their trouble, and he rescued them from their distress.

Bible Journaling Prayers

Adding notes to the pages of Bibles is something Christians have been doing since Bibles have existed in printed form. Prayers, insights, definitions, explanations, questions, and artwork—all have found a way onto the pages. These expressions are a way of engaging with the text and sharing our thoughts, prayers, and insights.

Over the last few years, Bible journaling has become a way to dig deeper into Scripture through creativity. This resurgence of decorating Bibles is based on the age-old practice of illuminating manuscripts with vivid color and imaginative art. Bible notes have again become pieces of art, and color is being added with paint, markers, and stickers.

Megan Wells of makewells.com shares how Bible journaling has impacted her prayer life:

I've opened my Bible almost every day since I started Bible journaling! At first, it was just because it was a new, interesting place to paint. But, slowly I started letting the words sink in again. And now I can truly say that lately I've been excited to hear what He has to say to me that day. It's a much better place to be! Of course, I'm not saying that painting in my Bible was the cure-all to my relationship with God, but I do think He knew just the thing that would get me listening to Him again.

Praying is not just about taking our concerns and requests to God. It is also about trusting Him with our worries no matter what the day brings. In Matthew 8:23–27, Jesus calms a storm that has scared the spit out of the disciples. He reminds them to trust Him. Writing these kinds of reminders in our own words, in our own creative way in the pages of our Bibles, helps us remember His promises.

Lord, I want to be like the winds and sea that are Yours to command. Replace my worry and anxiety with trust and calm. Show me places in the Bible that help me connect better with the real You. Amen.

Because he bends down to listen,
I will pray as long as I have breath!

PSALM 116:2 NLT

Practice your Bible journaling here.

. . . .

. . . .

. . . .

. . . .

. . . .

. . . .

. . . .

. . . .

. . . .

. . . .

. . . .

. . . .

. . . .

. . . .

. . . .

. . . .

. . . .

. . . .

. . . .

. . . .

Thank You, God, for always speaking to my heart.
I want to hear Your voice.
Help me put the world on mute so I can hear You.
Help me prioritize my days so there is time for You.

Practice your Bible journaling here.

I will give them a heart to know Me,
for I am the LORD; and they will be My people,
and I will be their God, for they will return
to Me with their whole heart.

JEREMIAH 24:7 NASB

Practice your Bible journaling here.

A godly prayer life has many dynamics.
Praising. Asking. Listening. Confessing.

JENNIFER GERELDS

Practice your Bible journaling here.

Prayer Walks

Prayer walks can be a great way to spend time with God. But what exactly is a prayer walk? It can be a simple walk outdoors that includes intentional prayer time while surrounding ourselves with His creation—alone or with a prayer partner or family member. A common practice on short-term missions trips is to walk through a city to pray for its people and churches.

According to Bree Zeitlin from faithfullycommitted.com, "A prayer walk is just like it sounds! You take a walk through a building or area, praying over each part as you go. This can involve thanking God, asking for blessings, and requesting protection."

Try taking a prayer walk through your home.

How do you do that? One area at a time. Bree suggests starting on the outside of your home, praying over each window and doorway. Include the garage and walkways. Then the house as a whole. Move to the inside of your home and pray over each room, for the family members and visitors who spend time in those rooms, for the activities that happen there.

Prayer walks can be a one-time thing or a daily thing. On the following pages are check boxes for the areas of your home and Scripture suggestions for each area. Read, pray, and check off each area as you pray through your home. Write your prayers on the remaining lines, or make checkboxes for each week or month to check off as you pray throughout the year.

Heavenly Father, thank You for my home. Thank You for every room, every window, every person, for the million little things that make this house a home. Lord, be the center of my home and the blueprint for my life. Amen.

God bless

this *home*

and *all* who enter.

☐ Pray for protection and peace over **doorways and windows**.

(2 THESSALONIANS 3:3, 2 SAMUEL 22:3–4, HEBREWS 12:14, PHILIPPIANS 4:6–7, JOHN 14:27)

☐ Pray for blessing and protection of those coming and going by **garages and walkways.**

(DEUTERONOMY 28:6, ISAIAH 41:10, ISAIAH 54:17)

....

....

....

....

....

....

....

....

....

....

....

....

....

....

....

....

....

....

....

....

....

....

....

....

....

☐ Pray for your **entire house** to be built on a firm foundation, physically and spiritually.

(MATTHEW 7:24–27, 1 CORINTHIANS 3:11, JOSHUA 24:15, PSALM 104:5, ISAIAH 33:6)

☐ Pray for provision, nourishment, and togetherness in the **kitchen and dining room**.

(MATTHEW 6:31–32, MATTHEW 4:4, JOHN 4:13–14, JOHN 7:37–39, MATTHEW 18:20, ACTS 2:42)

☐ Pray for each family member to be protected, to have peace, rest, and unity in **bedrooms**.

(JOHN 3:16, EPHESIANS 6:10–18, MATTHEW 11:28–30, PSALM 4:8, GALATIANS 5:22–23, MATTHEW 19:6)

☐ Pray for your **living and family rooms** to be welcoming, peaceful, and a place where everyone feels supported.

(ROMANS 12:18, 1 PETER 4:9–10, HEBREWS 13:2, EPHESIANS 4:15–16,
1 THESSALONIANS 5:11)

☐ Pray that your work is blessed in the **office** and that it never replaces your worship of God.

(COLOSSIANS 3:23, DEUTERONOMY 16:15, 2 CORINTHIANS 9:7, 1 TIMOTHY 6:10, MATTHEW 6:24, HEBREWS 13:5)

☐ Pray that in the messiness of life, God watches over you in **bathrooms, laundry rooms, and mudrooms**.

(GENESIS 28:20, JOB 29:2–3, PSALM 26:6–7, PSALM 51:2, LUKE 7:22)

World Prayers

Praying for the people of the world, for foreign governments, for missionaries—in your nation or around the world—is part of a robust prayer life. Some people pray for these things daily, some weekly, some monthly. Some pray as global issues arise.

A creative way to pray for the world is to include research about each country, read a book, watch a movie or documentary, or try food from that part of the world. As part of that emphasis, gather information on the countries you are praying for. List the countries or major regions. What are the main cities? The issues? Do you know missionaries there? Are there catastrophes that need prayer? Governments that are failing? People groups who don't know Jesus?

For example, if you were praying for Uganda for a week, start by searching the Internet or your local library for information about the country. Watch the documentary *Maria Prean* about the woman who became a missionary to Uganda in her sixties, or find a video about the animals who live there. Look for recipes you can make at home or find restaurants that offer Ugandan food. If you are crafty, try weaving a Ugandan basket, or go to a museum or gallery that offers art from Uganda. And all the while, pray for the country. By immersing yourself in the facts, sights, feel, and smell of the country, it will be imprinted on your heart.

Thank You, Jesus, for caring for all the people of the world. I pray for unity around the globe, for people to reach out to their neighbors across the world as well as across the street, for compassion and thoughtful action. Create in me a heart for the people of the world. Amen.

Ugandan Rolex
(Rolled Eggs)

This is a common street food found in Uganda that is traditionally wrapped in newspaper and eaten while walking.

Ingredients

2 eggs

¼ cup green cabbage
  (thinly sliced)

¼ cup tomatoes
  (seeds removed and finely diced)

1 tbsp shallot (minced)

Salt (to taste)

Olive oil or butter for cooking

1 large chapati (or any flatbread)

Sliced tomatoes, peppers, or other
  veggies for topping

Instructions

1. Crack eggs into a large mug. Add the cabbage, tomato, shallot, and salt. Stir until well combined.

2. Preheat a griddle or large skillet over medium-high heat. Oil well.

3. Add the eggs and spread out into a flat circle with the back of a spoon. Cook until set and bottom is browned.

4. Flip and cook another couple of minutes with chapati on top to warm.

5. Remove from pan and, when cool enough to handle, roll it up*.

*OPTION: Before rolling, you can add sliced tomatoes, peppers, or other veggies.

God shapes the world by prayer. The more praying there is in the world the better the world will be, the mightier the forces against evil.

ST. TERESA OF CALCUTTA

I'm not asking you to take them out of the world,
but to keep them safe from the evil one.

JOHN 17:15 NLT

This gospel of the kingdom will be preached in the whole world
as a testimony to all nations.

MATTHEW 24:14 NIV

To get nations back on their feet, we must first get down on our knees.

BILLY GRAHAM

A to Z Prayers

How would our communities change if we didn't just say, 'I'll pray for you,' but we actually did pray—deeply, intensely, and purposefully?" asks Amelia Rhodes in her book *Pray A to Z*.

Amelia discovered a creative way to help her to pray consistently. She created a system of praying through topics in alphabetical order. Instead of having a long list of individual prayer requests that she sometimes couldn't quite finish, she started praying by topic. "A is for adoption, B is for bullying, C is for cancer…"

Not knowing how to pray or what to pray sometimes keeps us from praying at all. With this creative alphabetical approach to prayer, there is always a prayer starter. You can check out the topics in Amelia's book or make your own A to Z list on the following pages.

For those creatives who want more, why not make a journal or notebook that is your Prayer Alphabet Book? Start with the letter A in calligraphy, stencil, cut from a magazine, stamped, or painted. Then write prayers about the topics that begin with that letter. When you get to the end, you will have an amazing prayer guide that you can use over and over or hand down as a family keepsake. If you have a friend going through a difficult time, consider creating a Prayer Alphabet Book filled with your prayers for him/her and offer it as a gift when you're done.

Heavenly Father, thank You for every blessing from A to Z. Help me use the alphabet as a way to connect more intimately with You and to pray for the people in my life, community, and nation. Show me creative ways to include the prayer requests that are entrusted to me in my daily prayer life. Amen.

A B C D E

F G H I J K

L M N O P

Q R S T U

V W X Y Z

The power of prayer is truly awesome. I know personally that when I put it off, my day isn't as purposeful and fulfilling. Having set prayer times can make it so much easier to stay consistent.

JESSICA AUTUMN

Never stop praying.

1 THESSALONIANS 5:17 NLT

I'm so thankful that we can pray in any place, position, posture, or situation. There is NO limitation on prayer—except not doing it!

MELANIE REDD

Pray in the Spirit on all occasions with all kinds of prayers and requests.
With this in mind, be alert and always keep on praying.

EPHESIANS 6:18 NIV

Coloring Prayers

Coloring relaxes most people. Studies show that when people color, their heart rate decelerates, their mind calms, and even their breathing slows down. Our bodies respond in a similar way during prayer or meditation. Coloring allows us to switch off parts of our brains and focus instead on the task in front of us. It is different from other art forms that demand you to think outside of the box, reroute thoughts, and pay attention. It is kind of like listening to music. It helps you relax and let go.

Since coloring produces such a state of tranquility, it is the perfect time to pray as your mind is already quieted by the activity. Next time you sit down to color, meditate on the good things God has put in your life. Ask Him to fill the time with encouragement and direction. Then listen to what He is speaking to your heart.

Use the picture you're coloring as your stopwatch; pray until it's complete. Pray for the things that have been stressing you out. Pray for peace and rest and relaxation. Or if you are using an inspirational coloring book, use the words on the page you are coloring as a springboard for your prayers.

Dear Father, thank You for giving me rest. Lord, help me to unplug, relax, and let go. Some days I have a hard time talking to You because I am too busy or too frustrated to stop and let Your presence comfort me. Show me how to use coloring, drawing, or other creative activities to slow down and to switch my focus to You. Amen.

I ONCE WAS *lost*, BUT NOW I'M *found*; WAS BLIND, BUT NOW I SEE.

Amazing Grace
John Newton, 1779

Prayer can never be in excess.

C. H. SPURGEON

Fair are the *meadows*,
Fairer still the *woodlands*,
Robed in the *blooming*
garb of *spring*.

Fairest Lord Jesus
Munster Gesangbuch, 1677

In quietness and trust is your strength.

ISAIAH 30:15 NASB

CROWN HIM
Lord of all.

All Hail the Power of Jesus' Name
Edward Perronet, 1779

I drove away from my mind everything capable of spoiling
the sense of the presence of God.

BROTHER LAWRENCE

NOTHING IN MY HAND I BRING, SIMPLY TO THE CROSS I CLING.

Rock of Ages
Augustus M. Toplady,
1776

This is the way/DAY/PAGE Sarah
Brought me this Book 11/28/22 McPike

Find a quiet, secluded place…. Just be there as simply
and honestly as you can manage. The focus will shift
from you to God, and you will begin to sense his grace.

MATTHEW 6:6 MSG

O how bright, THE PATH GROWS from day to day.

Leaning on the Everlasting Arms
Elisha A. Hoffman, 1887

The Prayer Closet

"You long to live a life focused on the things that truly matter and to find abundance in a simple life that's centered around God and your family," says blogger Katie Bennett. "And yet, you are frustratingly distracted and overwhelmed by busyness and all the trivial stuff of life."

Your phone, the television, the kids, work, chores, friends, errands, family… Finding time for prayer between the necessities and pleasures of life is flat-out hard. If you find time, you can't focus. If you focus, you are interrupted. What's a person to do?

"Consider creating your very own prayer closet to help you do that! This is something I have found beneficial in my distracted life, to be able to pray more like I want to," Crystal Reddick writes on Katie's blog embracingasimplerlife.com.

According to Katie's blog, making a prayer closet is as simple as the following:

1. Find space that is not being used and is big enough for you to sit or kneel.
2. Equip your space with a light, a throw pillow, or an afghan to make your time comfortable but not sleep inducing.
3. Gather photos of your family and friends to tape to walls or keep in small albums so you can have visuals to pray over.
4. Include a Bible and highlighters or pencils to mark verses as you read.
5. Keep this prayer journal in the closet so you can write down prayer requests and answers, check off prayer lists, make notes, etc.
6. Spend a portion of your time actually on your knees, fully seeking God.
7. Set a timer so you won't be distracted with worry about going over time.
8. Pray with a sincere and open heart.

Lord, You know me inside and out. I am trying to be transparent and real but that is so hard with everything that is going on around me. Show me where I can put time in my day and a place in my home that is dedicated solely to You. I want You to be the focus of my day. Amen.

Prayer
is not learned

in a classroom,

but in the *closet.*

E. M. BOUNDS

I learned how to fight in prayer first.

ALEX AND STEPHEN KENDRICK

When you pray, go into your inner room, close your door
and pray to your Father who is in secret, and your Father
who sees what is done in secret will reward you.

MATTHEW 6:6 NASB

The reality is, my prayers don't change God. But, I am convinced prayer changes me. Praying boldly boots me out of that stale place of religious habit into authentic connection with God Himself.

LYSA TERKEURST

Jesus got up and went out to an isolated place to pray.

The Lord's Prayer

Perhaps the most famous prayer in the world is the Lord's Prayer from Matthew 6 and Luke 11. When asked how to pray, Jesus taught the disciples this prayer. Even though it may be the most recited prayer in the world, we can expand it for a more meaningful, creative prayer experience.

Dissecting the prayer into smaller parts for daily emphasis is something The Church of the Highlands in Birmingham, AL, encourages. There are seven main sections that give guidance to your prayer life, one for every day of the week:

1. *Our Father:* As you walk into God's presence, give honor to Him, the Father of all creation.
2. *Hallowed be Your name:* Praise Him with all your heart, rejoicing in His promises and remembering His faithfulness. Tell Him how thankful you are. Sing. Worship. Rejoice.
3. *Your will be done:* Pray for His will to be revealed to you, for doors to open or close to indicate the way to go. Spend time listening to His still, small voice.
4. *Our daily bread:* Your heavenly Father knows your needs, and He will provide for them. Ask in faith for both for your own needs and those of others. Be specific.
5. *Forgive us our debts:* Ask God to forgive you. He longs to give you this gift. Offer the same forgiveness toward any who have offended you. Forgiveness heals.
6. *Lead us not into temptation:* God's grace is our protection. Request a safety zone to keep temptation at bay and for strength to resist it if it breaks through.
7. *For Yours is the kingdom:* Pray for God's power and authority over your life. Thank Him for the blessings He brings in answer to your prayers.

Taking one aspect of the prayer for each day of the week, you can inject your prayer life with new energy. Or simply draw or write the words from the original prayer as you pray each day or on those days when prayerful words won't come. Try praying the Lord's Prayer in this new way for a week or a month. By exploring the prayer example given to us by Jesus, our prayer life will become deeper and more meaningful.

Our Father in heaven,

Hallowed be Your name.

Your kingdom come.

Your will be done

On earth as it is in heaven.

Give us this day our daily bread.

And forgive us our debts,

As we forgive our debtors.

And do not lead us into temptation,

But deliver us from the evil one.

For Yours is the kingdom

and the power and the glory forever. Amen.

MATTHEW 6:9–13 NKJV

Our Father in heaven…

Hallowed be Your name.

Prayer does not fit us for the greater work; prayer is the greater work.

OSWALD CHAMBERS

Your will be done...

Give us this day our *daily bread.*

Jesus said, "This is how you should pray."

LUKE 11:2 NLT

And *forgive us* our debts…

And do not lead us into *temptation*...

....

....

....

....

....

....

....

....

....

....

....

....

....

....

....

....

....

....

....

....

....

....

....

....

You are a child of your heavenly Father. Confide in Him.
Your faith in His love and power can never be bold enough.

BASILEA SCHLINK

For *Yours* is the *kingdom*...

My mouth is filled with Your praise and with Your glory all day long.

Checklist Prayers

For many people, checking items off a to-do list makes their day. Lists give guidance and structure. You know exactly what needs to be done and get a feeling of accomplishment when you check each item off the list.

Praying by lists is an organized way to pray for the people and issues in your life. Make lists that you want to remember daily (like family, work, health), weekly (like extended family, friends, upcoming events), or monthly (like missions organizations, government officials, world matters). Write the lists in your planner or journal, or put them in your phone with an alarm set as a reminder to keep praying. As things come up, add them to the appropriate list.

Making lists may not seem like the most creative way to pray, but here are some ideas for adding a creative flare. Journalers often design pretty pages with markers or colored pencils for the daily, weekly, or monthly lists in their planners or Bibles. By adding a pretty tab, these pages can be easily referenced over and over.

Another option is to write your lists on vellum or rice paper. When you put this opaque paper on top of a painting or drawing, the art will show through. Then position both under glass on a desk or table, or in a frame set near your workspace so you will see them daily.

You could also simply tack the lists to a corkboard with fun embellishments, write them on a framed chalkboard, or jot them down the side of your bathroom mirror with a dry erase marker. Lists can be fun!

Heavenly Father, thank You for showing me the miraculous organization You brought to the universe. You have ordered the timing of the seasons, structured the cells in our bodies, and shown us through the Bible the value of organization. Help me utilize prayer lists in a way that is pleasing to You and fun for me. Amen.

Prayer Requests

☐ ....
....
....

☐ ....
....
....

☐ ....
....
....

☐ ....
....
....

☐ ....
....
....

☐ ....
....
....

☐ ....
....
....

☐ ....
....
....

Prayer Requests

- [ ] ....
....
....

- [ ] ....
....
....

- [ ] ....
....
....

- [ ] ....
....
....

- [ ] ....
....
....

- [ ] ....
....
....

- [ ] ....
....
....

- [ ] ....
....

The more you pray, the more you will get done in your life.
It's crazy how that works, but it's so true.

Prayer Requests

- ☐ ....
  ....
  ....
- ☐ ....
  ....
  ....
- ☐ ....
  ....
  ....
- ☐ ....
  ....
  ....
- ☐ ....
  ....
  ....
- ☐ ....
  ....
  ....
- ☐ ....
  ....
  ....
- ☐ ....
  ....
  ....

Let's get organized.

JEREMIAH 8:14 MSG

Prayer Requests

- [ ] ....
  ....
  ....
- [ ] ....
  ....
  ....
- [ ] ....
  ....
  ....
- [ ] ....
  ....
  ....
- [ ] ....
  ....
  ....
- [ ] ....
  ....
  ....
- [ ] ....
  ....
  ....
- [ ] ....
  ....
  ....

The most efficient use of an overfilled day is to spend the first hour in prayer.

Prayer Requests

- [ ] ....
....
....
- [ ] ....
....
....
- [ ] ....
....
....
- [ ] ....
....
....
- [ ] ....
....
....
- [ ] ....
....
....
- [ ] ....
....
....
- [ ] ....
....
....

I'll make a list of God's gracious dealings,
all the things God has done that need praising.

Singing Prayers

$\mathcal{S}$inging prayers to God is something all the Judeo-Christian religions have in common. Whether of the Jewish, Catholic, or Protestant tradition, each use music as a way to offer praise to God. You may have heard the adage that singing is like praying twice! Many times, it is the most sacred or traditional prayers that are sung, not spoken, during the religious service. But we shouldn't let that limit us to singing prayers only when we're at church or exclusively during holidays or festivals. We can sing our praises and prayers to God any time, in our own way, in our own voice.

One way to praise God through music during your prayer time is to sing the prayers that you have sung in church or heard on the radio. Some churches start services this way every time they meet. The Lord's Prayer, "Praise God from Whom All Blessings Flow," or songs from Handel's *Messiah* are beautiful examples. To make this part of your personal time with God, find the lyrics, play the music, and sing along. Consider buying songs on your smartphone and creating a playlist of just prayer music. Join your soul with the words and sing them to God.

Another way to sing prayer is to put your own words to melodies you know by heart. The Bible says, "Sing a new song to the LORD!" (Psalm 96:1 NLT). For example, singing to the tune of "Mary Had a Little Lamb," the Star Wars theme, or "Ode to Joy" can frame words like "Jesus, help me through today, through today, through today…" Off the cuff or carefully crafted, these songs can become a beautiful link between you and the God who created music.

I love You, Lord. And I lift my voice to praise You. Thank You for music and melodies. I want to sing words that are sweet to Your ears. Amen.

Let them *sing*

joyful *praises* forever.

PSALM 5:11 NLT

Sing, O heavens; and be joyful, O earth;
and break forth into singing, O mountains:
for the LORD hath comforted his people.

ISAIAH 49:13 KJV

This is my story, this is my song,
Praising my Savior, all the day long.

FANNY CROSBY

Sing to him, sing praises to him; tell of all his wondrous works!

1 CHRONICLES 16:9 ESV

Then sings my soul, my Saviour God, to Thee;
How great Thou art, how great Thou art!

CARL BOBERG

Labyrinth Prayers

A labyrinth is a spiritual tool that has been used by religious groups for thousands of years. One famous example, the labyrinth at Chartres Cathedral in France, was constructed in the thirteenth century and is more than forty-two feet wide. A labyrinth is a guide for a contemplative walk to the center of a circular path and back out. When paired with a faithful heart and sincere prayer, it can become a creative exercise that brings us closer to God.

"It is not a maze, but a single path that leads to the center and back," says author Kathryn Shirey on kathrynshirey.com. "It will twist and turn, but you will not get lost. Walking the labyrinth can be experienced as a metaphor for your own spiritual journey with all its twists, turns, and meandering. The point is not to figure out how to get to the center, but how to take the next step with God."

As you begin your labyrinth prayer walk, quiet your mind and prepare your heart for getting nearer to God. Concentrate on thanking Him for the blessings in your life and releasing the thoughts and frustrations of the day. Once you arrive in the center, ask Him to be the center of your life. Take a moment to listen to what He is saying to your heart. As you walk out of the labyrinth, ask for guidance and for His presence to go with you wherever you go.

To experience a labyrinth at home, build one out of rope or garden hoses in the backyard. Or "walk" one with your fingers using the drawings on the next few pages. Your labyrinth can be as simple as a chalk drawing on the garage floor or as complex as hedges and plants. Be creative and do what works for you.

Dear Father, thank You for walking with me. Help me to center myself in Your love and grace. Help me to follow Your path and listen to Your heart no matter how many twists and turns I encounter in life. Help me to trust You to always know the way. Amen.

This image is a drawing of the labyrinth on the floor
of the Chartres Cathedral mentioned on the previous page.

....
....
....
....
....
....
....
....
....
....
....
....
....

It is solved by walking.

ST. AUGUSTINE

There is no God like you in all of heaven and earth. You keep your covenant and show unfailing love to all who walk before you in wholehearted devotion.

The task of spiritual direction is not to make something happen,
but to become aware of what God is already doing, so that we can respond to it,
participate in it, and take delight in it.

LISA A. MYERS

How blessed are those whose way is blameless,
Who walk in the law of the LORD.

Prayer and Fasting

asting is a spiritual exercise that can be misunderstood. The purpose is to abstain from something for a period of time, to sacrifice one thing so you can better focus on another. It is the practice of letting go of something you enjoy as a way to detach from worldly things. You can fast for a day, a week, or a month. Although fasting most often refers to abstaining from certain or all foods, you can fast from things like social media, the coffee shop, or television.

The key to all fasting is prayer. Replace the thing you are removing from your life with prayer time. Or take the discomfort and offer it up as a form of sacrifice for a particular prayer intention or request. Spend time with God. Seek His guidance and direction. Use the hunger or withdrawal from a habit to become more aware of the needs of others or to be more tuned in to God's presence.

Many people are afraid to fast because they aren't sure they can do it, or they don't know how, or they think it is only for the super religious. It isn't. The relationship with God you get from fasting is available to everyone. (If you have medical concerns, please consult your physician before starting a fast.)

The overall point is to put yourself in a little bit of an uncomfortable situation and see how God responds to you. If you have never fasted before, start small. Commit to fasting a cup of coffee each day or giving up sweets during the week. When you reach for the coffee or your taste buds want sugar, pray. You can use each discomfort for a specific prayer intention. For example, when you need another cup of coffee, pray for the friend who needs more focus in her life. Or when you would kill for a cookie, pray for your friend with diabetes.

Once you've successfully fasted one thing, move on to maybe skipping one meal a day for twenty-one days or unplugging from social media for a month or sleeping without a pillow for a few weeks. Historically, people fast when they are waiting to hear from God on an issue. The fasting amplifies the prayers as we empty ourselves, literally and figuratively, in this way.

Conduct your fast in creative ways: Make a chalkboard chart, decorate a list in your journal, download a fun app to your phone, or use the chart below to mark off each day of your fast. Or make a countdown calendar similar to an Advent calendar that you can open each day to a small surprise like stickers, pens, paint, yarn, needles, or whatever inspires your creativity.

Dear heavenly Father, thank You sacrificing so much for me. Make me strong and dedicated enough to fast and pray. Build my faith in You and my reliance on You. When I am weak, Lord, bring to mind all the ways You show me love. Amen.

We fasted and earnestly prayed that our God would take care of us,
and he heard our prayer.

Fasting is more about replacing than it is about abstaining—replacing normal
activities with focused times of prayer and feeding on the Word of God.

GARY ROHRMAYER

When you fast, put oil on your head and wash your face, so that it will not
be obvious to others that you are fasting, but only to your Father.

MATTHEW 6:17–18 NIV

A fast is not a hunger strike. Fasting submits to God's commands.

Envelope Prayers

*C*reating envelope prayers is another way to explore new options for praying. Some people keep all the prayers they pray for a week or a month in envelopes, then read them to see which need further prayer and which can go into an ANSWERED envelope.

Some people put the prayer requests of others in an envelope, then pray holding it in their hands as they engage God on the other person's behalf.

Another fun way to use this system is to label envelopes with prayer prompts like THANK YOU, PLEASE, SORRY, HEALTH, FINANCES, or PROTECTION. Or FAMILY, HOME, CHURCH, WORK, FRIENDS, or WORLD. As you go through your days, write names or situations on paper and put them in the appropriate envelopes. For example, THANK YOU might have something as simple as "the sunrise was amazing" or "coffee completes me." WORLD could have things like "safe elections" or "freedom for innocents." Then at the end of the week, empty the envelopes and thank God for those prayers or renew the requests as needed.

The envelopes can be simple, small white envelopes or they can be homemade, decorated, and fancy. Use envelopes that engage you in the activity. Keep slips or a pad of paper readily available so you can jot down requests and add them no matter where you encounter a need. It is a creative and organizational method of keeping track of prayer in a beautiful way.

Dear Lord, help me think outside the envelope when I pray. Thank You for the opportunity to pray for others in creative ways and to carry them in my heart as I go through my day. Lord, use me to make a difference for the people You have put in my life to love, nurture, and share the world with. Amen.

Prayer is a powerful privilege.

ALEX AND STEPHEN KENDRICK

I urge you in the name of our Lord Jesus Christ
to join in my struggle by praying to God for me.

ROMANS 15:30 NLT

The more you pray, the less you'll panic.
The more you worship, the less you worry.
You'll feel more patient and less pressured.

RICK WARREN

God…is my witness as to how unceasingly I make mention of you,
always in my prayers making request.

ROMANS 1:9–10 NASB

Sermon Note Prayers

"The challenge with creative note-taking," lettering artist and author Krystal Whitten explains in her book *Faith & Lettering*, "is that the message is different every time. There aren't any hard-and-fast rules, and you never know what you're going to end up with on paper. But the creative challenge is part of the fun and beauty of it, and ultimately, it'll enhance your lettering and listening skills."

Sermon notes also give structure to prayer if you follow a few simple tips:

Listen.   Process what you hear, but don't try to write down every word the speaker says. Just record the main ideas or what stands out to you.

Write.   Write quickly and legibly. Concentrate on getting the words down, not on drawing elaborate letters. The time to embellish is later.

Draw.   But don't let it distract you from listening. Leave a space to come back and finish later.

Pray.   Look over the words you've captured and say them as prayers.

Lord, open the eyes of my heart so that I can better understand You. Help me to show my love for You by loving the people I interact with every day. Fill me with Your Spirit so I can better understand Your direction and find my purpose. Thank You for calling me to You and giving me hope. Amen.

DATE

I pray that the eyes of your heart may be enlightened in order that you may know the hope to which he has called you, the riches of his glorious inheritance in his holy people.

EPHESIANS 1:18 NIV

SERMON NOTES: ....

....

....

....

....

....

....

....

....

....

....

....

....

....

....

....

....

....

....

MY PRAYER: ....

....

....

....

....

....

Practice your sermon note art here.

Every artist dips his brush in his own soul,
and paints his own nature into his pictures.

HENRY WARD BEECHER

DATE

SERMON NOTES: ....

....

....

....

....

....

....

....

....

....

....

....

....

....

....

....

MY PRAYER: ....

....

....

....

....

....

Practice your sermon note art here.

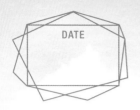

DATE

We are God's masterpiece.

EPHESIANS 2:10 NLT

SERMON NOTES: ....

....

....

....

....

....

....

....

....

....

....

....

....

....

....

....

....

....

....

MY PRAYER: ....

....

....

....

....

....

Practice your sermon note art here.

He listens well who takes notes.

DANTE ALIGHIERI

DATE

SERMON NOTES: ....

....

....

....

....

....

....

....

....

....

....

....

....

....

....

....

....

....

MY PRAYER: ....

....

....

....

....

....

Practice your sermon note art here.

Psalm 119 Prayers

Psalm 119 is the longest psalm and also the longest chapter in the Bible with 176 verses. The verses are divided into twenty-two stanzas, one for each letter of the Hebrew alphabet. Some Bibles include the letter before the stanza, others do not. *The Book of Psalms for Creative Journaling* not only includes the letter, it also includes the name of each letter.

Because of the way this psalm is organized, it affords us the opportunity to use a unique technique for prayer. Translate the name of the person you are praying for into Hebrew through a translation program, such as doitinhebrew. com. Once you have the Hebrew letters, find the equivalent symbol/letter in Psalm 119. Then read or write those stanzas as a prayer for that person.

For example, we translated Ellie Claire. The translation into Hebrew is אליקלייר, read right to left. The names of the Hebrew letters in *Ellie* are (א)aleph, (ל) lamed, (י) jod in *Claire*: (ק) koph, (ל) lamed, (י) jod, (י) jod, (ר) resh. So to pray for Ellie Claire, you would read Psalm 119:1–8 (aleph), 89–96 (lamed), 73–80 (jod), 145–152 (koph), (repeat lamed and jod if you like), and 153–160 (resh). The names for the symbols in this case correspond with the King James Bible. Newer Bible translations spell some of the alphabet letters with slight variations.

Try this system with your name or your husband's, kids', friends', or parents' names. Once you have their verses, either read or write them, or write a prayer using words from the corresponding verses you've found. For example, if you were praying for Ellie based on Psalm 119 it could sound something like this:

Father, thank You for putting Ellie in my life. Please help Ellie to walk in the way of the Lord, to seek You with her whole heart, to follow Your commandments, to praise You. Ellie is Yours. Save her. Help her to understand Your Word and desire Your will for her life. I pray that Your mercy and kindness will be with her all the days of her life and that she will wholeheartedly follow You. Amen.

Hebrew Alphabet

ה	ד	ג	ב	א
He (H)	**Daleth** (D)	**Gimel** (G)	**Beth** (V/B)	**Aleph** (Silent)
י	ט	ח	ז	ו
Jod (Y)	**Teth** (T)	**Cheth** (KH)	**Zain** (Z)	**Vau** (V)
ם	מ	ל	ך	כ
Final Mem* (M)	**Mem** (M)	**Lamed** (L)	**Final Caph*** (KH)	**Caph** (K/KH)
פ	ע	ס	ן	נ
Pe (P)	**Ain** (Silent)	**Samech** (S)	**Final Nun*** (N)	**Nun** (N)
ר	ק	ץ	צ	ף
Resh (R)	**Koph** (K)	**Final Tzaddi*** (TZ)	**Tzaddi** (TZ)	**Final Pe** (P)

*Denoted here by the word "Final," the letters *Caph,*
Mem, Nun, Pe, and *Tzadi* have an alternate form
when they are at the end of a word.

ת	ש
Tau (T)	**Schin** (S/SH)

NAME:

NAME: ....

....

....

....

....

....

....

....

....

....

....

....

....

....

....

....

....

....

....

....

....

If we truly love people, we will desire for them far more than that
which is within our power to give them, and this will lead us to prayer.
Intercession is a way of loving others.

RICHARD J. FOSTER

NAME:

NAME:

I have hidden your word in my heart.

PSALM 119:11 NIV

NAME:

NAME: ....

....

....

....

....

....

....

....

....

....

....

....

....

....

....

....

....

....

....

....

....

....

If there has come to us the miracle of friendship, if there is a soul to which
our soul has been drawn, it is surely worthwhile being loyal and true.

HUGH BLACK

NAME:

NAME: ....

....

....

....

....

....

....

....

....

....

....

....

....

....

....

....

....

....

....

....

....

....

....

....

Listen to my prayer.

PSALM 119:170 NLT

NAME: